WORD FROM THE EDITOR

In a world where divisiveness has turned into religion, it's never been more important to be tolerant. The world does not have to be filled with hate and we should strive to build a better world for the next generation. This month, in the midst of chaos and in the absence of Pride, let's think on what tolerance means for us and when it has been absent in our lives. Why is it so important or, more controversially, why isn't it? Share your stories and creative expressions with us. We firmly believe it will help cultivate tolerance, even if it's just an ounce.

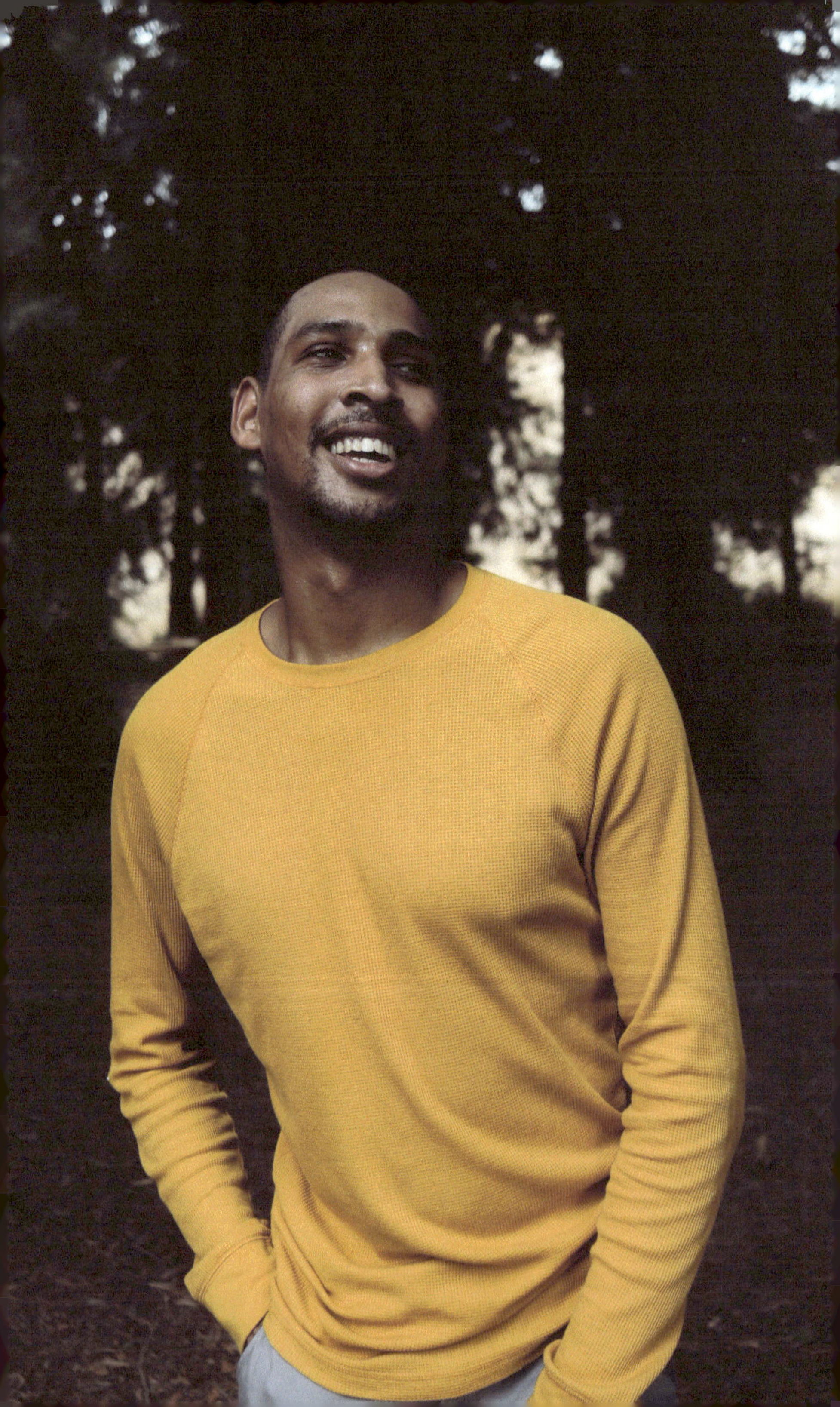

Photograph *by Josephine Jael Jimenez*

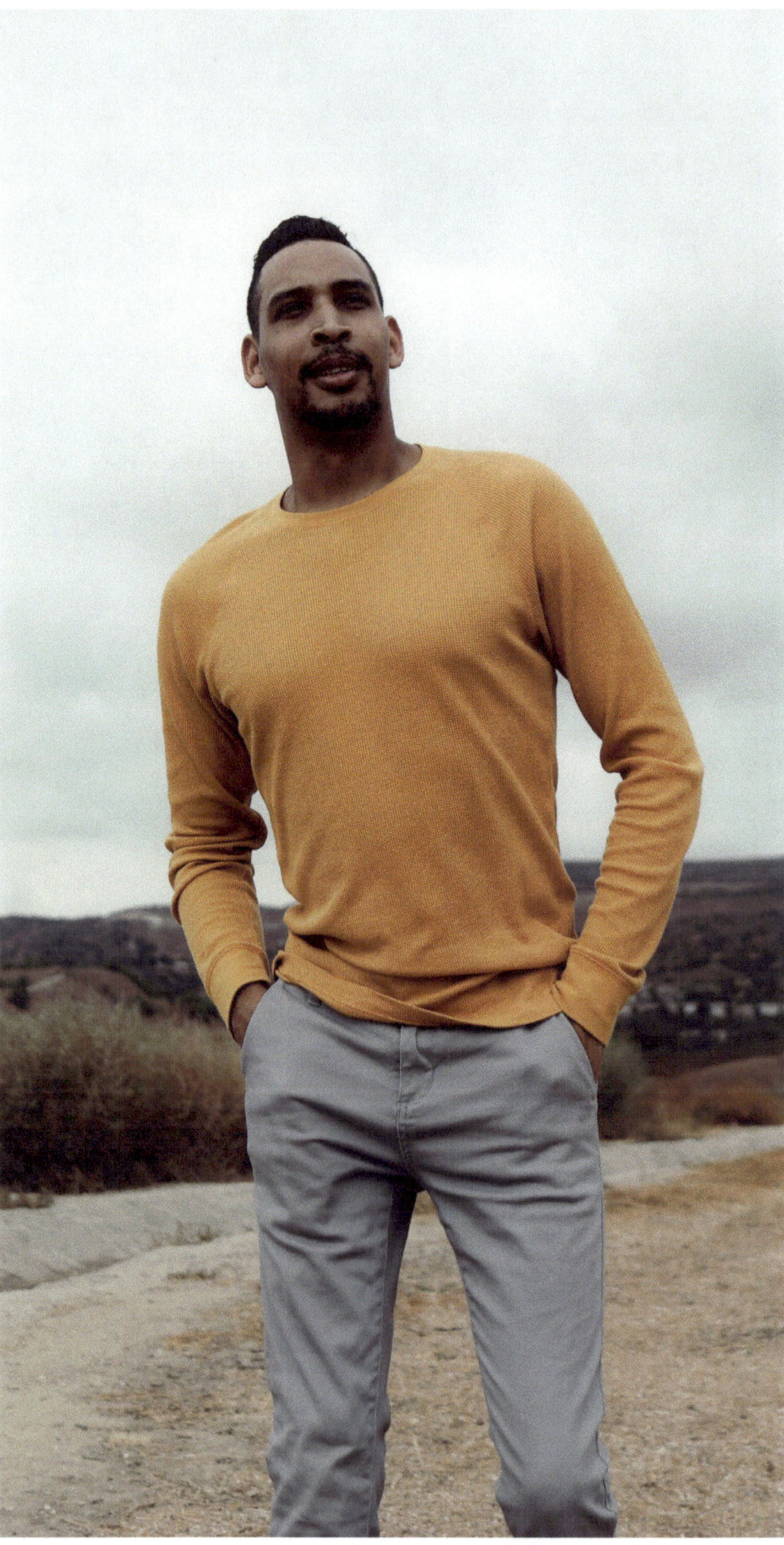

ALONG THE NARROW ROAD

AN INTERVIEW WITH DISABILITY ADVOCATE GEORGE RAMIREZ

BY JOSEPHINE JAEL JIMENEZ

When George walks down the street, most people will immediately notice that something is different about him. They'll see an impeccably dressed young man walking down the street with shoes that may or may not have scuff marks in odd places. Maybe they'll even notice his huge smile and his cheerful demeanor, but they most definitely will notice the way he walks.

When George was young, doctor's told his mother that he would never walk. They said that his brain may not have received enough oxygen during pregnancy and permanent damage was done to his muscular system. He was diagnosed with cerebral palsy.

Cerebral palsy is defined as a group of permanent movement disorders that become clear in early childhood. The symptoms of cerebral palsy vary from person to person, and can be categorized by the different way it affects the body. Some experience poor coordination, stiff and/or weak muscles and tremors. Other symptoms include issues with sensation, speech, vision, hearing, and swallowing. Basically, it can show up in any part of the body in any way imaginable.

George's mother never accepted it when the doctor's said he would never walk. Instead, she personally handled his physical therapy and pushed him to stand and walk using

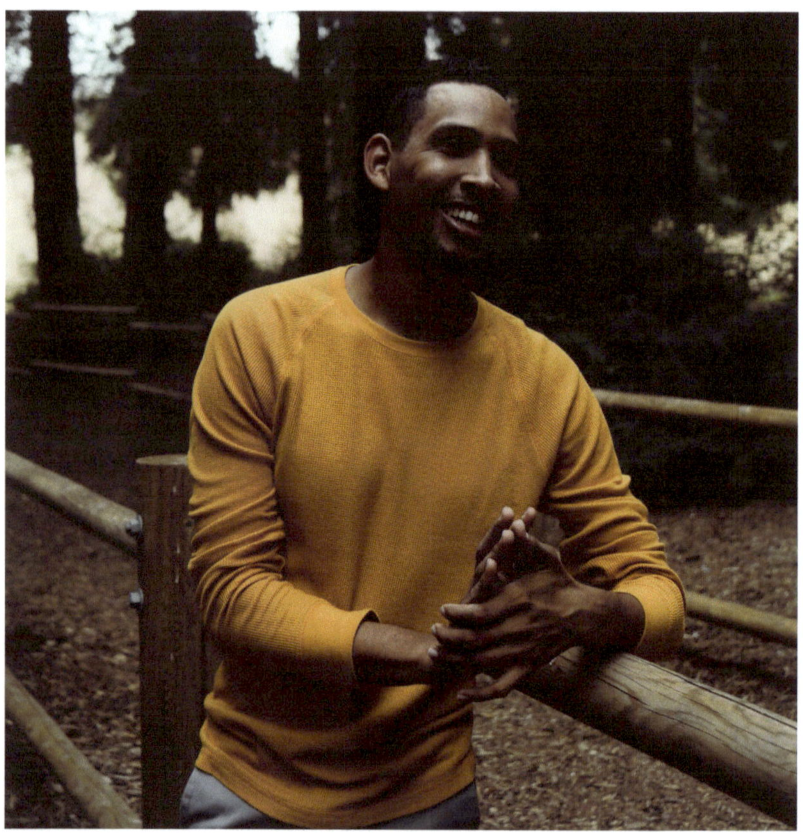

a walker. By the age of 5, he was able to walk on his own. His gait may not be that of every other person walking down the street, but he can walk. He's grateful for that.

"When I look back at all that," said George, "I think that's where my definition and my view on tolerance comes from. It started with my mom and her ability to say, 'They said this about you, but we're going to prove them wrong.'"

Despite what the doctor's told his mother about his diagnoses, George doesn't really blame them for what they said about him potentially not being able to learn how to walk. When he was born, there wasn't a lot known about CP. Others who shared George's diagnoses weren't able to walk or talk, so he doesn't think it was an unfair assumption on their part. But the assumptions that came after were what really held the potential to veer him off his life's path.

For whatever reason, people tend to associate physical disabilities with mental disabilities. They treat it as if your leg muscles working differently meant that your brain did, as well.

In grade school, George's teachers thought he might have a learning disability because he wasn't doing great in school, so they held him back a year. It wasn't until after the next school year started that they realized he didn't actually have a learning disability, he was just lazy. The difference in George's situation compared to other kid's was that because of his physical disability, his teachers and school made the assumption that he wasn't progressing because he probably had a learning disability based on the way he walked.

These types of assumptions have never stopped showing up in George's life. Ever since he started applying for jobs at the age of 16, he was always judged based on his disability. Jobs would like what they saw on paper only to immediately write him off as soon as he stepped into the room. No matter the type of job, they always assumed that he was less capable because of his gait.

George doesn't let his disability stop him from doing the things he likes and wants to do. He works out regularly, by lifting weight or going on hikes, and is even considering trying to start modeling. He doesn't try to hold himself back in any way because he knows his limitations are not as abundant as people want to think. In a recent conversation, he had to go so far as to defend his education. Someone he was speaking to was thoroughly surprised when George mentioned that he had earned a Bachelor's degree. Not one to shy away from challenging people's perceptions, George asked him why he was so surprised.

"He didn't have an answer. So in my mind, it's either one of two things or both. It's either surprising because of the fact that I'm disabled or the fact that I'm a person of color," said George.

This person said it was good that he had a degree, but in a way that didn't sit well with George. It wasn't enough that they were surprised, they expressed how good it was that Georfe had a degree with a sense of awe and pity that most disable people know so well. It's good that George was able to achieve something he shouldn't have been able to achieve.

What George couldn't understand about this person's question is why they didn't expect someone like him to have a degree. Why did they feel the need to praise the fact that he had a degree? Isn't it good for anyone to have a degree? This person felt the need to affirm a disabled person of color for achieving what middle class white young adults are expected to achieve. This person didn't expect someone like George to have a bachelor's degree, so he felt the need to give him an attaboy as if his praise meant something to George. As if George should feel grateful for this man's praise and for noticing that he was actually capable after all.

"I will always have to defend myself and the fact that I have an education because it's not expected as someone with a disability." said George. "People look at me and think that I'm not capable or that I should not be capable of obtaining a bachelor's degree or any degree in general."

He was proud that he was able to get his degree, but he felt tired of having to explain that pride to people. He feels like he has to answer for that pride, like it was different that what anyone who graduated from college would feel.

"Why do we set limits for people? And why do we set the bar so low? Why should that be a question and why do I constantly have to endure [answering] that question or statement," said George. "I wonder what it would take to change people's mindset about disabled people and the other stigmas that people have."

The discrimination that George and other people with disabilities feel is not all their heads. 33% of employers say that they do not hire people with disabilities because they believe they cannot perform the required job tasks. And what could be a result of this discrimation is that only 35% of people with at least one disability of working age have a job and the poverty rate of people with disabilities, which is about 47%. Only 45 countries in the world today have anti-discrimation laws that are aimed to help protect individuals with disabilities.

But despite these statistics, George wants people to know that you can be successful and have a disability.

"People with physical disabilities are successful. And I believe the reason for that is that we're tired of people putting us in categories. We have to fight our way out to achieve and succeed," said George. "I have a friend who is a pro-surfer and he has CP. He walks worse than I do and he can surf! My friend Katherine is wheelchair bound and she's a writer on [an established TV show]. A lot of my friends have masters degrees and careers."

George's aim is to shift the narrative around success and disabilities and he believes it starts with being mindful and asking thoughtful questions. Instead of saying, "Oh, you have a degree?" say, "What's your degree in?" He wants people to start with questions before labeling people and putting them into boxes.

"I think we [as disable people] need to start speaking up," said George. "I think we, myself included, have given ourselves too many passes because, let's be honest, having a disability can be an advantage. We can say we don't want to do something because of our disability. People aren't going to start looking at us differently until we tell them to. It's that point where we have to say, 'Enough is enough. Stop making assumptions about us.'"

"One of my mottos is, 'If I can't do something, I'll tell you,' said George. 'Until then, don't assume that I can't. If I need help, I'll let you know.' I've struggled a lot with identity and confidence and owning who I am as an individual. Now that I'm getting older and immersing myself in my disability and others like me, I'm learning to understand that it's okay for me to be myself, it's okay for me to speak up and it's okay for me to have a voice. It took me a while to get over the hump of, 'What will people think about what I have to say.' But it doesn't matter. Because even if I'm 'wrong,' I'm entitled to my own experiences and my experiences are valid. So I'm learning to speak my truth and [to own] my experiences."

Currently, George is working on having his website and podcast up and running by the end of July, just in time for his birthday. Along the Narrow Road will educate people on CP and other disabilities in the hope of making the world more accessible.

Photography *by Josephine Jael Jimenez*

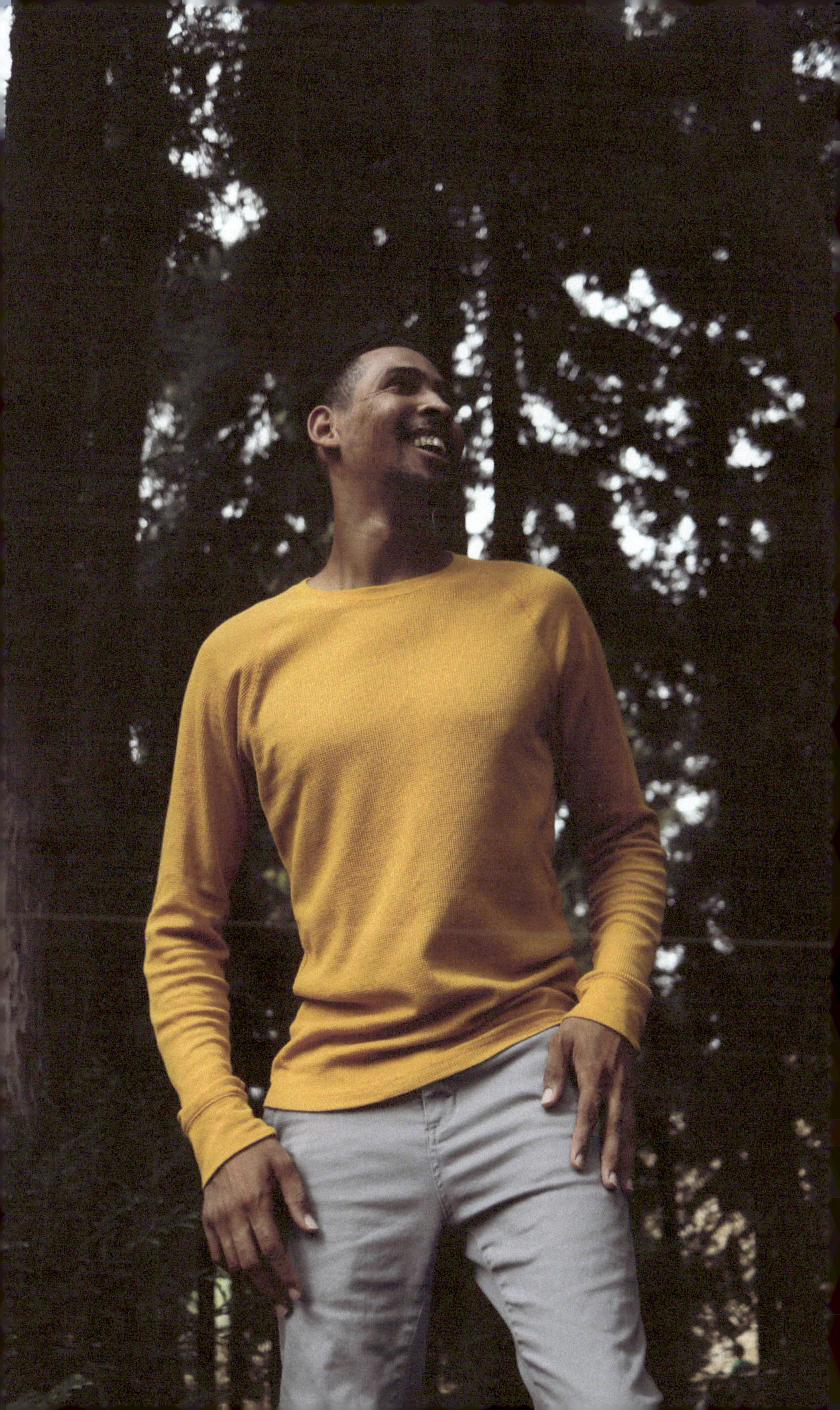

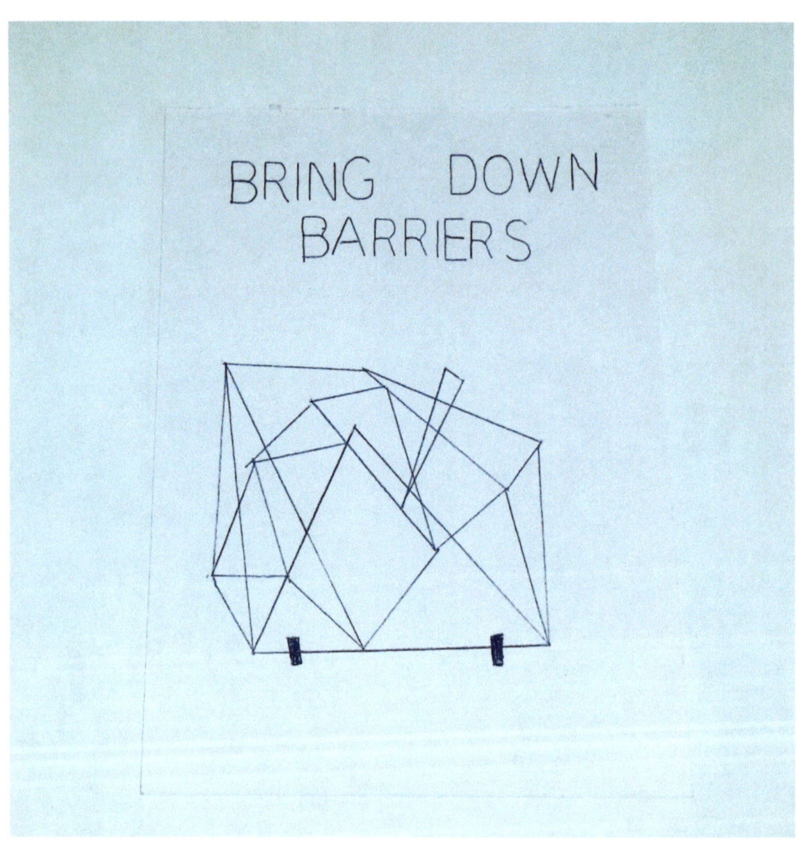

Textile art *by Teri Anderson*

CHANGE IS INEVITABLE

YURA SAPI

You've known it
for a long time coming

Thinking about what becomes a side mission
what has taken you off track for a minute here and
there

pulling you forward but inhibiting you for full force

just make it through for one more

one more plan

then back to the place you started it all

back to rebirth

replan the plan

redo the ideas

everything was supposed to happen the way it did,

but now it its time to face the truth.

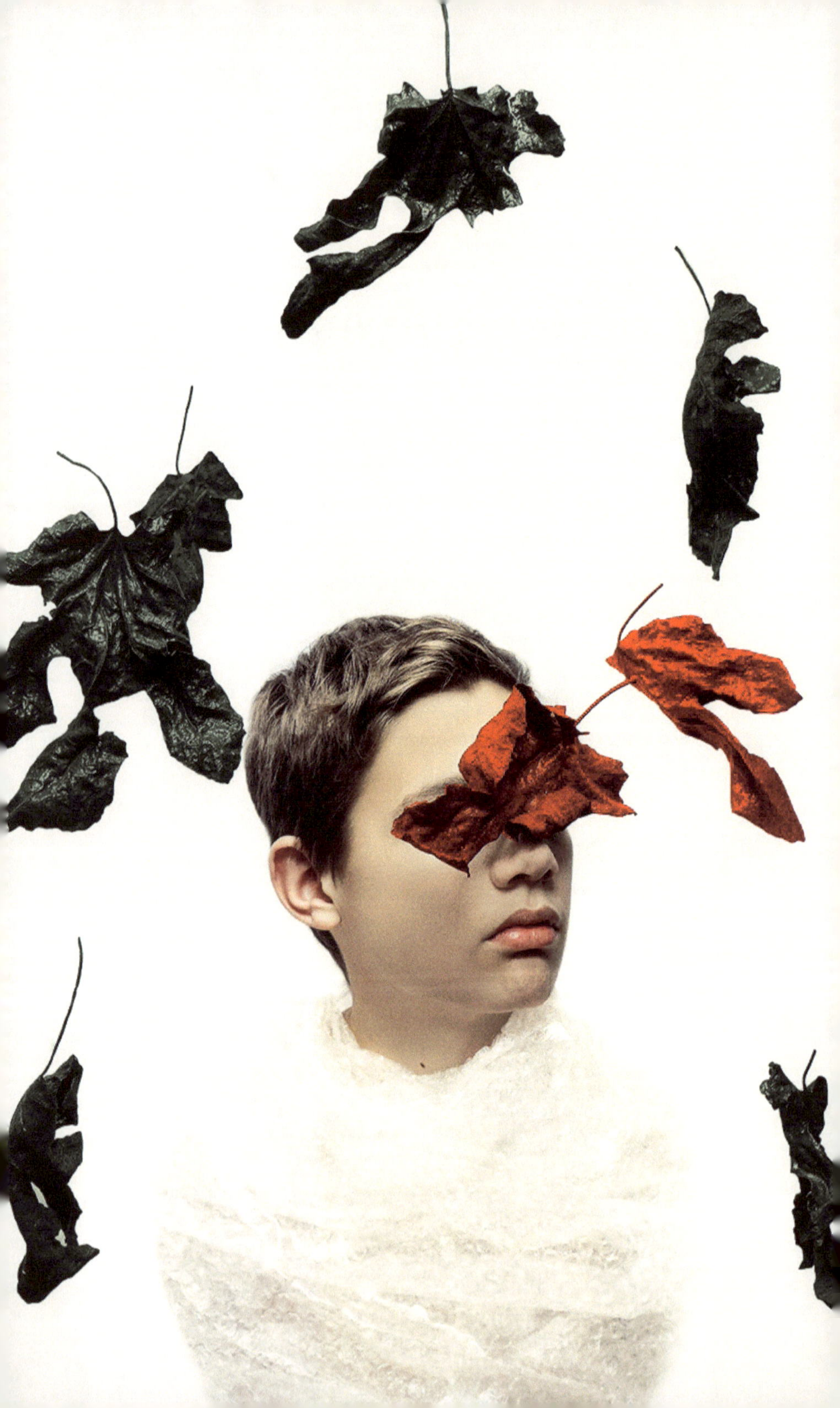

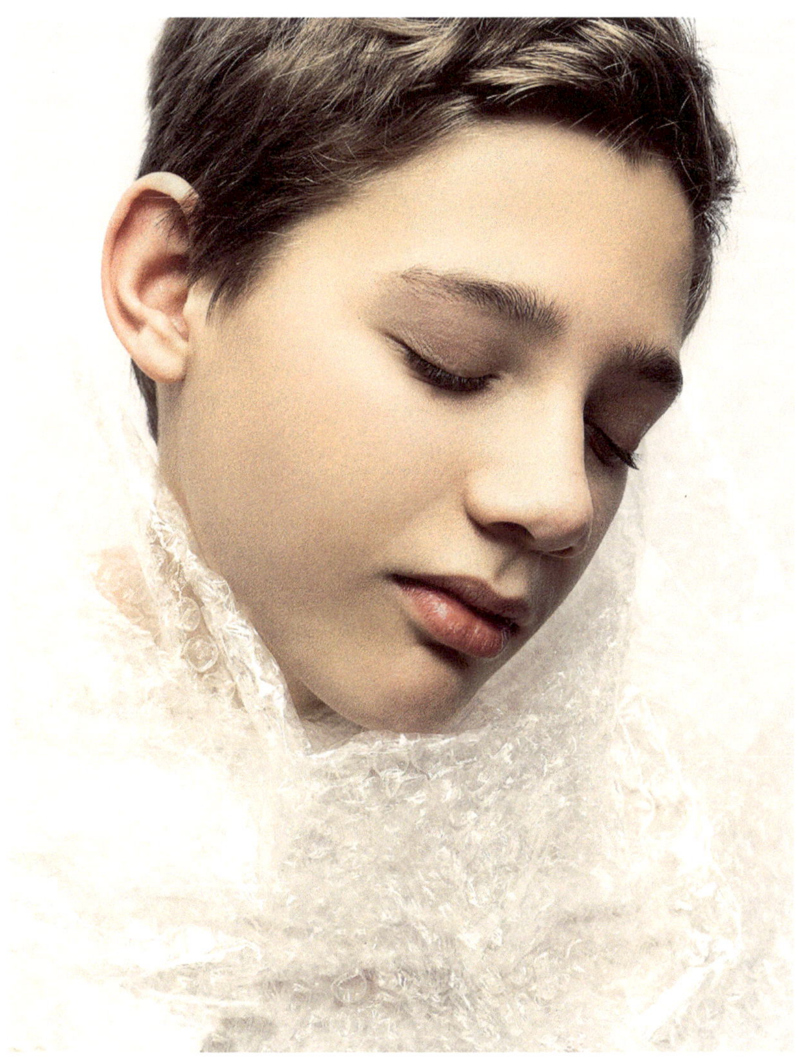

Photographs *by Pierre van Vuuren*

LOVE

MELISSA ARELLANO

We strive to stand out
to stand out together
all united
like one common feather
But we aren't so common
different colors, shapes, and sizes
with some hiding under disguises,
of the same matching face.
We are beautiful in our differences,
and our differences make us beautiful
In our perceptions
and our common misperceptions.
in our differences lie stories that we can share
to entertain, enlighten
and sadden different readers
with which we have not in common other than our genus.

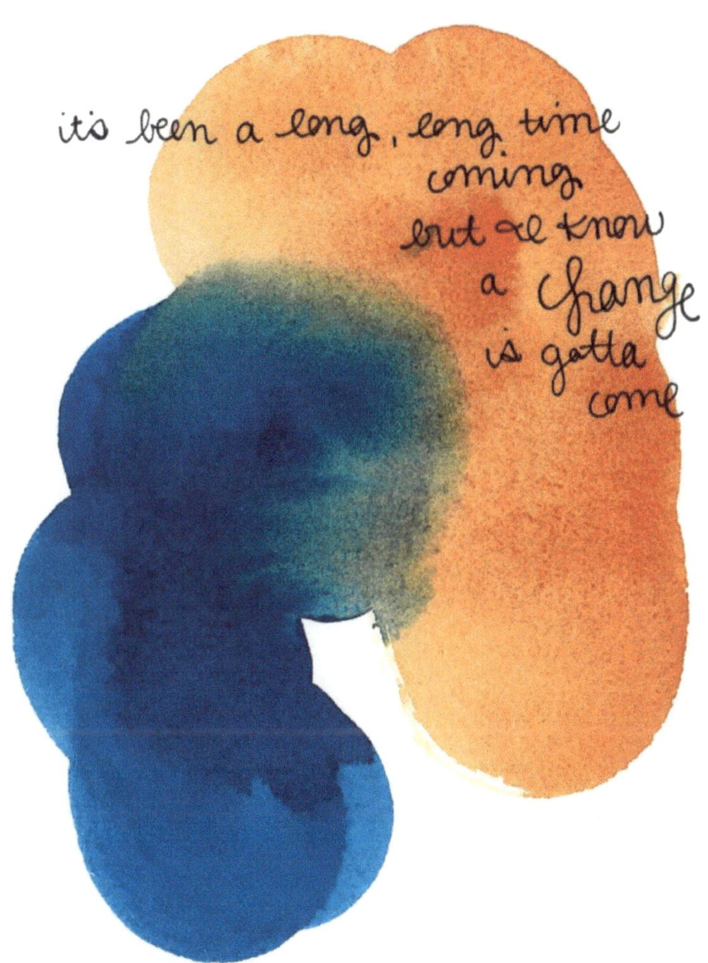

Doodle *by Josephine Jael Jimenez*

black lives matter

throwback to a playlist by will hawkins
for YI's RECLAMATION issue

OPTIMISTIC.....SOUNDS OF BLACKNESS
KING KUNTA.....KENDRICK LAMAR
KEEP YA HEAD UP.....2PAC
MORE BOUNCE TO THE OUNCE.....ZAPP
OUTSTANDING.....THE GAP BAND
ALRIGHT.....KENDRICK LAMAR
BLACK.....INNANET JAMES
WHERE THIS FLOWER BLOOMS.....TYLER, THE CREATOR
WHEN THE REVOLUTION COMES.....THE LAST POETS
DON'T TOUCH MY HAIR.....SOLANGE, SAMPHA
VRY BLK.....JAMILA WOODS FT. NONAME
GONNA BE A LOVELY DAY.....KIRK FRANKLIN, THE FAMILY
LAND OF THE FREE.....JOEY BADAS$$
FDT.....YG, NIPSEY HUSSLE
DNA......KENDRICK LAMAR
THIS IS AMERICA.....CHILDISH GAMBINO
CROWN.....RAPSODY
STAND TALL.....CHILDISH GAMBINO
HOLY.....JAMILA WOODS
SOMEDAY WE'LL ALL BE FREE.....DONNY HATHAWAY

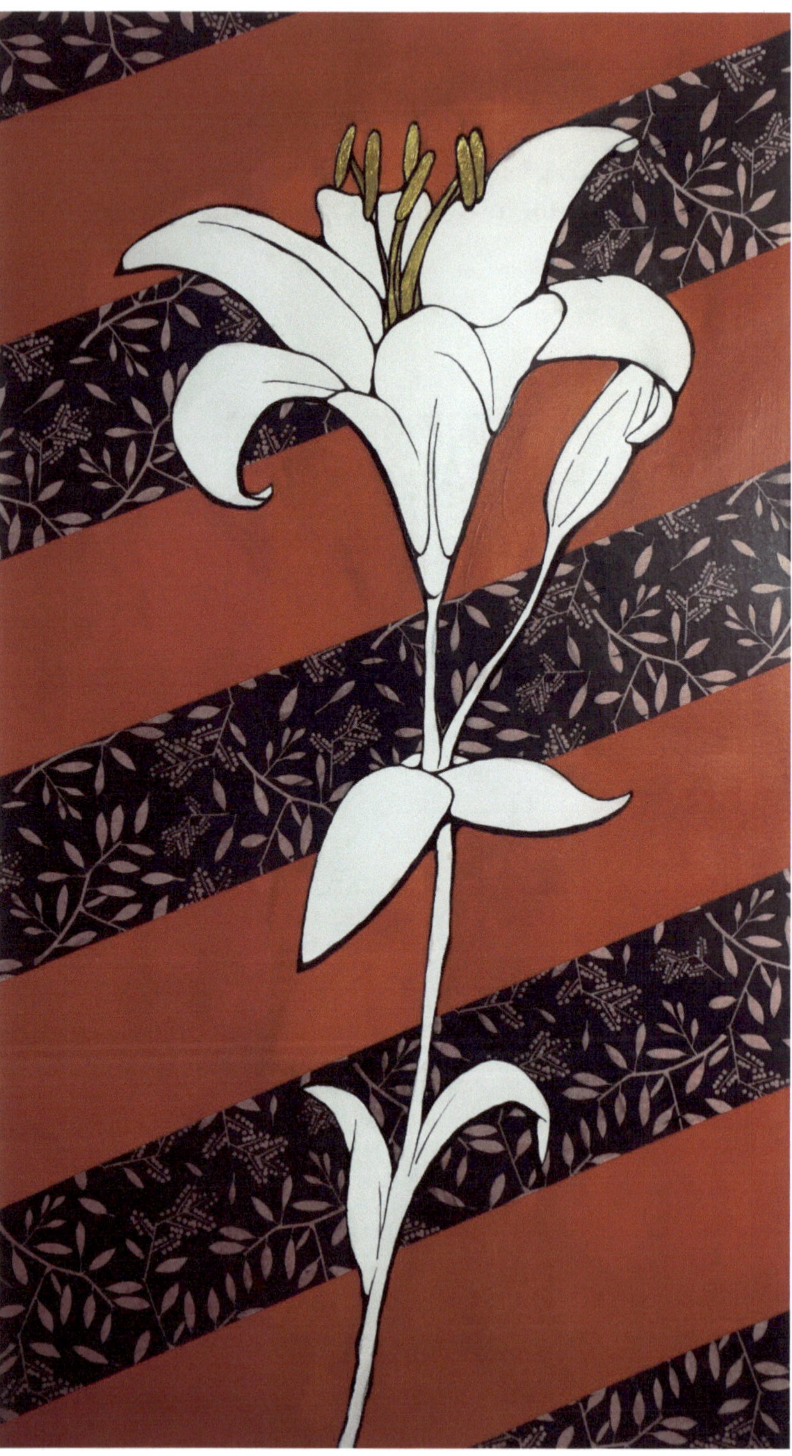

TOLERANCE IS A COP-OUT!
IMARI REDE

It's just one step in the right direction
One small step
That still leaves room for a
Mental war, waging that
"They" will never be enough

It allows for hate to live
Silently in the brush
Lurking in the background
Feeding chisme

And continuing to divide

It feels like a cookout
where you are invited and
expected to show face

All you get to eat up
Are the disarming words
And your drink is made
Of tears, forced to swallow

On the verge of bursting
You find your worth and decide to leave
Then, I /we /you no longer have to pretend

That you're okay with
My life choices,
With who I really am
The person I've grown to be

Painting *by Gilberto Zuniga*

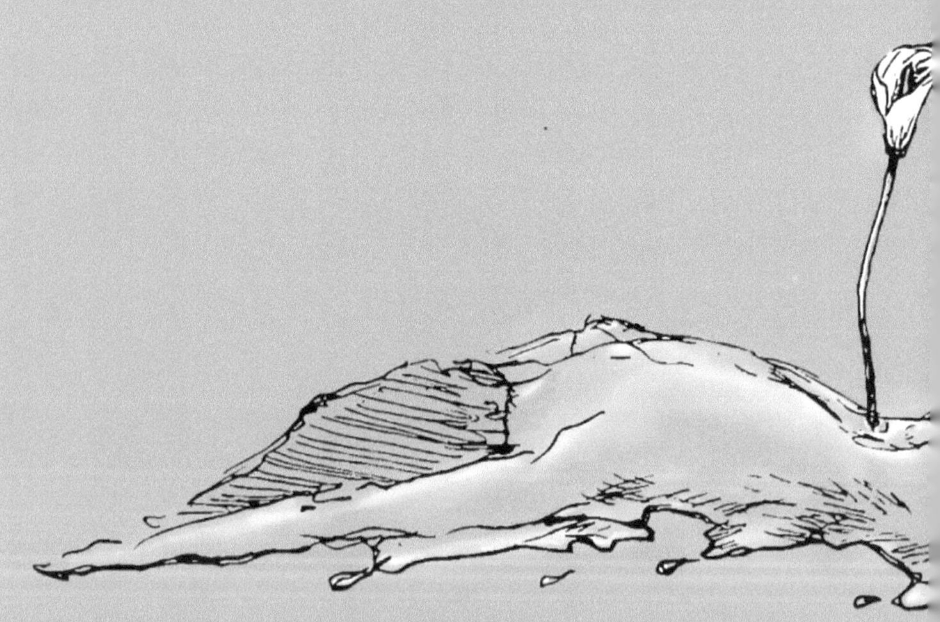

"life from death" *by Violet Del Cid*

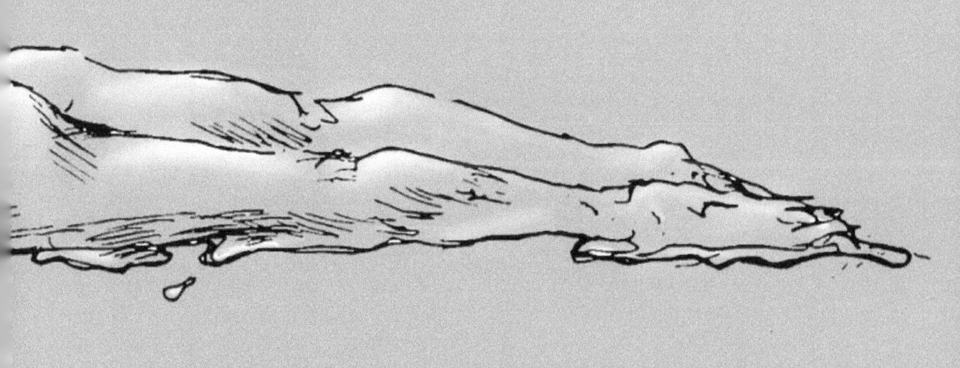

THE VICE COLUMN

tolerant/ intolerant

Josephine Jael Jimenez

I'm pretty woke, both objecticely and subjectively. I do the work to keep myself informed and I fight against injustice often enough for my parents to call me whenever there's a protest on LA's streets.

Over the years, I've considered my tolerance for people to grow. I don't unfriend Trump supporters and I let some asshole white guy comment on my Facebook posts without engaging. I have argument after argument with people to try to convince them there are better ways to be living through life. Recently, however, I've come to realize that maybe I'm not so tolerant after all.

I can't stand people that chew with their mouths open. I hate when I see children running around wild while their parents are on their phone, clearly unconcerned with the safety of their child. I hate whiny bitches at Disneyland complaing to workers about shit they can't fix. I'm ready to fight ANYONE who tells someone not to speak Spanish in America. That last one might be justified, but I talk a big game about being tolerant enough to have productive conversations. Some instances don't warrant a conversation from me, at least not in my head.

Worse yet, I'm not tolerance of people I love being so set in their ways, they won't even entertain the notion that they may be wrong or that the world is evolving with or without them.

There's not a lot of gay people in my family. Sexuality in the religious Mexican culture is still contentious, but one of my cousins was brave enough to come out way before it was safe to do so.

My family is generally alright

about it. They didn't disown him or beat him or make him feel like less of a person, but they've definitely taken a page from the American playbook and decided to be passive aggressive about it. As a result, he's decided to go live his life in the big city of Guadalajara where he's not the odd guy out and where he was able to meet his life partner. Every year, he goes back to the family for exactly two days for Christmas and then he head on back home. That's about all the passive-aggressiveness and bad jokes he can handle for one year. I don't blame him. Our famliy can be cruel in ways that isn't always apparent to outsiders, but we know what they mean when they say, "We'll see what the Lord says at the gates of heaven." They send him to hell too often to be healthy for his sanity.

This year, he will be marrying the love of his life and our family will not be attending the ceremony. Hell, he might not have even bothered sending them an invitation. They've always said, since I can remember, that if he were to ever stop sleeping around and settle down, they wouldn't attend the wedding because it goes against everything they believe in.

I grew up in the religion that convinces my parents that attending a ceremony of love would be blasphemy and I left as soon as I was old enough to feel the intolerance seeping from the walls. My parents never felt the same inclination, but because I left, I've always told my father when he said he wouldn't be attending the wedding that it would be against his best interests to not attend. As his favorite kid and as the person who has him wrapped around his finger, he knows that his absence is going to cost him dearly. Why? Because I don't tolerate that shit. Lord knows if my child is gay, I will move heaven and earth to make sure that they do not have to deal with the same bullshit. I don't tolerate that shit because if my dad doesn't show up to my kid's wedding because he's gay, I'd cut him out of our lives in a heartbeat. And my dad and I are best friends. Thick as thieves. But I don't like people who break hearts for not good reason.

Maybe that's not really being intolerant. Maybe I'm not being as harsh as I think I am. Family has a way of getting under your skin and they're generally the ones I can't tolerate the most, but all I know is that even if I am being harsh, I don't really care.

I don't live in the camp that says that we must be tolerant of all. I'm never going to not punch a Nazi in the face and I'm never gonna let the KKK live their merry lives hunting after Black people. Tolerance is not a two way street. It's the radical notion that people should be respected for their humanity and all the parts that their humanity is: their sexuality, their gender identity, their race, their ethnicity, their culture. Tolerance is about the core part of a human being, not necessarily the beliefs that they learned in this life.

I'm glad my parents call me when there's a protest and I'm glad I stand up to my father when he's being even the tiniest bit homophobic because to me, it's the same fight. Maybe I really am as tolerant as I think I am.